Contents

Going to the dentist 4

In the waiting room 6

Meeting the dentist 8

The dentist gets ready 10

The check-up 12

Clean and polish 14

Brushing teeth 16

Problem teeth 18

Well done! 20

The next appointment 22

Index 24

Going to the dentist

Remember to give your teeth a good clean before your visit.

In the waiting room

What time is your appointment?

Tick, tock! Tick, tock!

There are lots of fun things to do while we wait.

Meeting the dentist

What do you think of my chair?

The light can go up and down and forward and backward.

9

The dentist gets ready

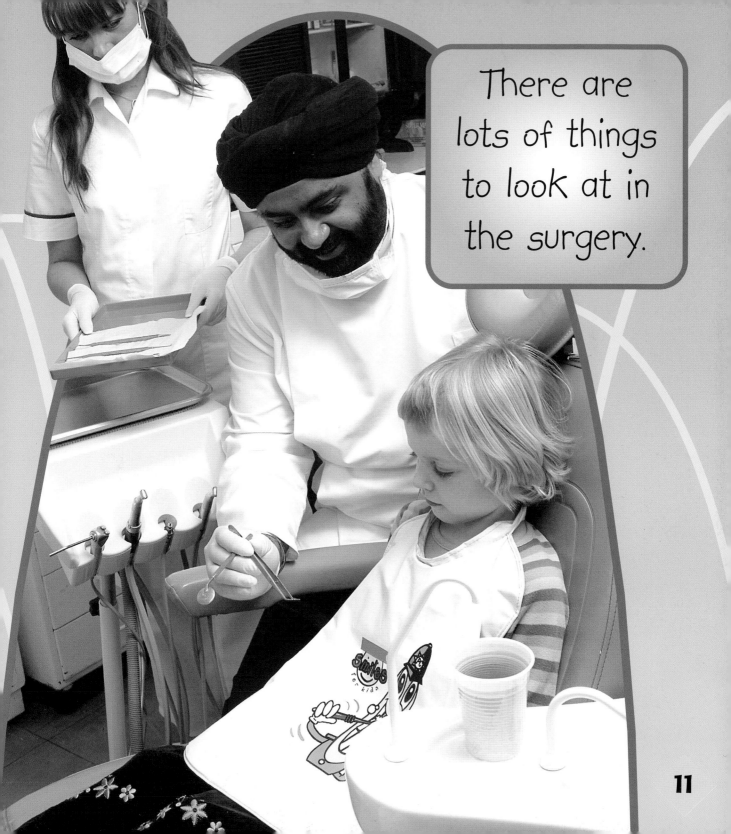

There are lots of things to look at in the surgery.

11

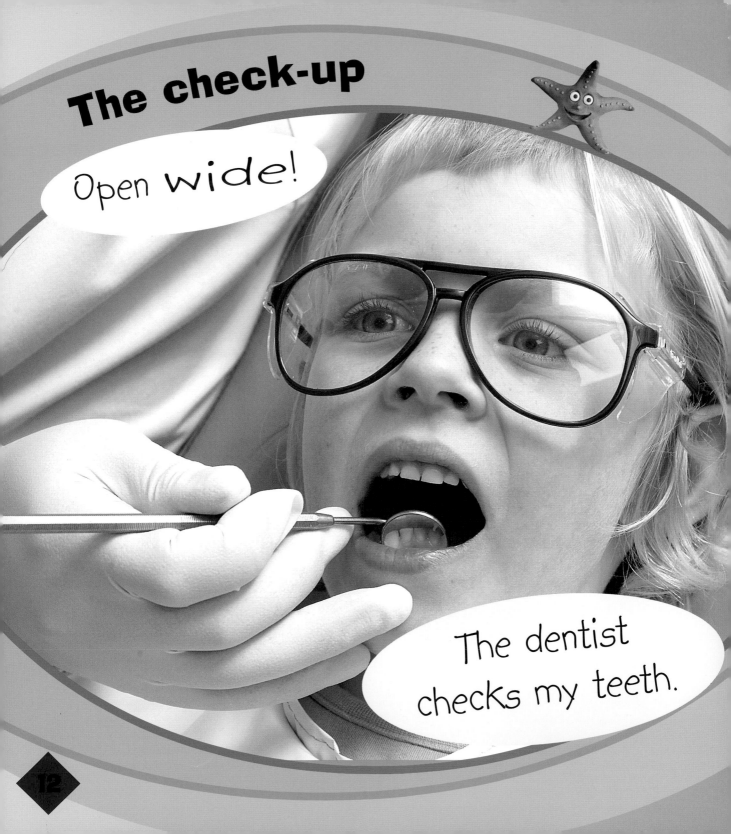

'All OK!', he says. The nurse writes up my notes.

Clean and polish

This is going to make my teeth really clean.

Bzzzzzzzzzzz! It feels nice and tickly!

Splat!

Time to rinse and spit!

15

Brushing teeth

The dentist shows me how to brush.

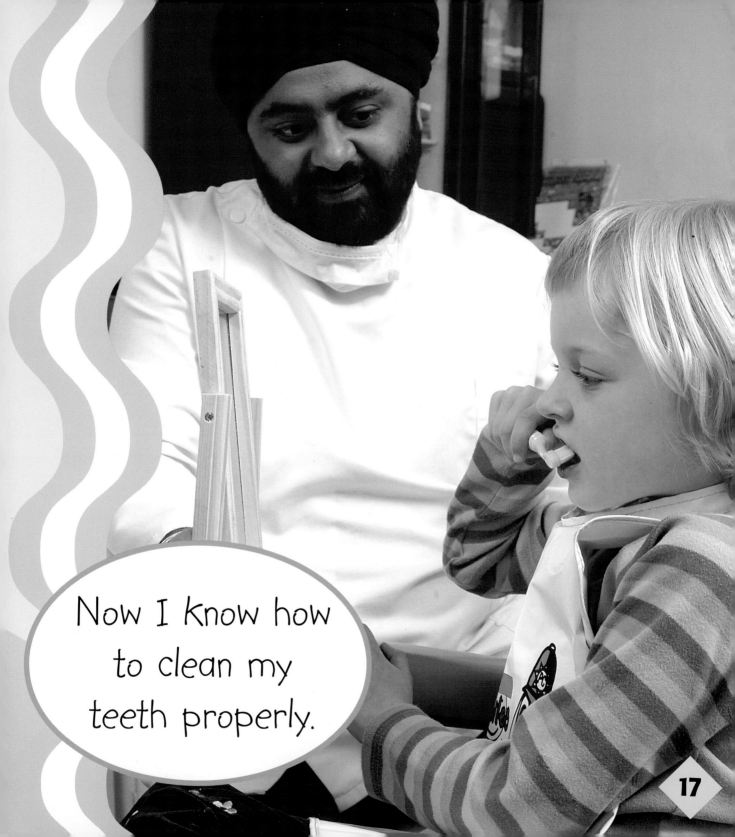

Now I know how to clean my teeth properly.

17

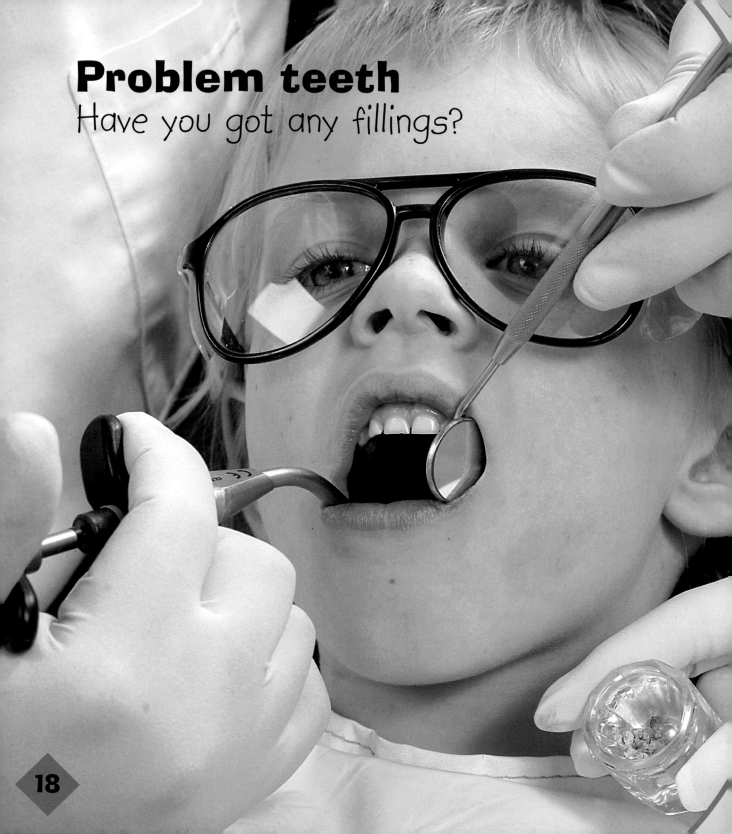

Problem teeth

Have you got any fillings?

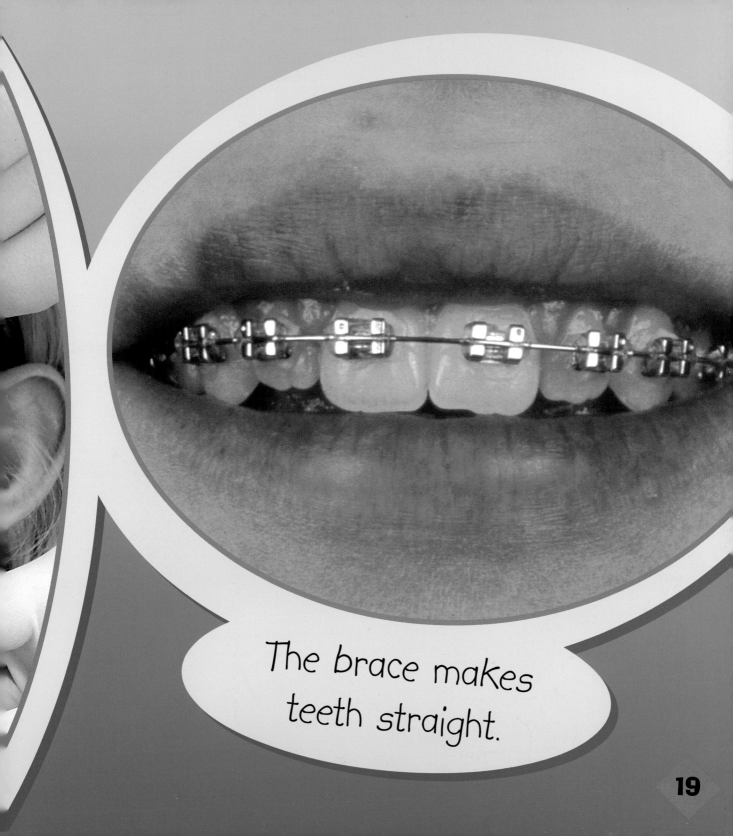

The brace makes teeth straight.

Can I have this toothbrush, Mum?

21

The next appointment

23

Index

appointment 6, 22

brace 19

brushing 4, 16, 17

dentist's chair 8

dentist's light 9

dentist's mirror 11, 12, 18

rinsing 15

stickers 20

toothbrush . . . 16, 17, 21

The end

Notes for adults

This series supports the child's knowledge and understanding of their world, in particular their personal, social and emotional development. The following Early Learning Goals are relevant to the series:

- respond to significant experiences, showing a range of feelings where appropriate
- develop an awareness of their own needs, views and feelings and be sensitive to the needs and feelings of others
- develop a respect for their own cultures and beliefs and those of other people
- manage their own personal hygiene
- introduce language that enables them to talk about their experiences in greater depth and detail.

Each book explores a range of different experiences, many of which will be familiar to the child. It is important that the child has the opportunity to relate the content of the book to their own experiences. This will be helped by asking the child open-ended questions, using phrases like: How would you feel? What do you think? What would you do? Time can be made to give the child the chance to talk about their worries or anxieties related to the new experiences.

Talking about the dentist
A visit to the dentist can seem less daunting if the young child has had the chance to watch a parent's teeth being examined beforehand. Parents can emphasize the fun of 'riding' in the dentist's chair, the tickling sensation in the mouth, spitting out and the sticker at the end! For those children who do have fillings the emphasis can be placed on the need to brush teeth regularly and avoid too many sweet foods and drinks.

Further activities
Follow-up activities could involve making a chart that can be ticked when the child has cleaned his/her teeth every morning and evening, perhaps using a new toothbrush and different toothpaste. It can also be fun to find which toys have teeth and to give each toy a 'check-up'.